WHY PROMPTS?

When I'm stuck on the page, I'll take twenty minutes or so and write on a prompt. It clears the cobwebs, keeps my pen moving, and I always get fresh ideas as a result of going off-road for a bit.

~LISA MCCULLOCH, NOVELIST

Creative prompts generate sparks that illuminate a path away from literary inertia.

~DARLENE JUNKER, RED OAK WRITER

Hearing a single word, phrase or series of words evokes a pause, but, then, like a dragster who sees the green light, my pen races along the blank sheet of paper with words, sentences, and paragraphs. None of which would have come had it not been for the suggestion.

~ALINE MOHR, POET

I felt completely capable of dreaming up things to write about. Who needs a muse? Then a friend showed up with a piece of flash fiction written completely in dialogue, which she said resulted from a writing prompt. Fascinating, I thought, and continued on my way. Later, I accidentally signed up for a class that included prompts. I surprised myself with the ideas and words that percolated out of my subconscious. I am *be-mused*.

~JO DEMARS, RED OAK WRITER

Prompts spark conversation, on the page or around the writers' table, and whether about craft or the writing life, a good prompt paves the way for connections.

~CHRISTI CRAIG, AUTHOR, TEACHER, PUBLISHER

THE PEN CALLS

The Pen Calls

KIM SUHR

RED OAK
writing

To the members of my
Time to Write! group,

Your courage at the page
&
generosity of spirit inspire me.

CONTENTS

Introduction

Dear Reader,

Before I would ever have courage enough to claim the label, "writer," I easily carried the identity of "reader." I suspect you do, too. (I mean, you're reading this letter, right?)

When I was a wee tot, my 15-year-old aunt, Jean Anne, who lived with us, ended up grounded for an entire summer (now, there's a story!)—grounded, that is, except for the freedom to take me to the Monroe Street Library, which, I'm grateful to say, she did with great regularity. These trips made me feel happy and at home surrounded by books. I imagine we read our way through the picture books in the collection. Dr. Seuss's rhyming and cadence still echo in my ears, and, every so often lo these 50+ years hence, Jean Anne will recite the "Once a leopard saw his spots..." rhyme to me (which is not Dr. Seuss and was actually in a book we owned rather than one from the library—but still).

What I remember with more specifics, though, are trips I made to the library when I was old enough to get there on my own and check out books with the cream-colored library card, my uneven, second-grade signature on the back. I can still hear the crinkle of plastic-covered books and the ka-thunk as the demagnetizing machine did its job, the stamp-stamp of the due date being inked onto the check-out card and the slip taped inside the cover. The squeaky wire rack of paperback *Peanuts* books, which featured comic strips of Charlie Brown, Lucy, and the gang—and which I read through, sometimes twice or three times in a summer.

Later, I exhausted the collection of Encyclopedia Brown and Little House books from the tiny library at the end of the hall at St. James School. Judy Blume entered my life, including the forbidden *Forever...*, in which teen sex had no negative consequences (gasp!), giving me new ways to see myself, my changing body, and my relationships with friends and guys. The girl who turned me onto Blume probably sneaked me the copies of *Dinky Hocker Shoots Smack!* and *Go Ask Alice*, too. Talk about forbidden.

What matters in all this is that books gave me mirrors and windows and doors into the world—and, since you're reading this, I bet they have done the same for you. The other thing I would bet is that, maybe more than once while reading a book, you have thought about what *you* might write, given the chance.

Well… here's your chance!

In my work as a writing instructor, I am consistently floored by the insights and memories that bubble up when people are sparked by a writing prompt and given the freedom to write without fear of judgement or criticism. They are surprised to unearth long-buried memories and delighted to see associations that their brain comes up with almost without trying.

So now, you, dear reader, hold in your hands a set of keys to unlock a latent writer inside *you*. I encourage you to grab a warm beverage, find a quiet corner, set a timer for 15 minutes, choose a prompt, and start writing—freely and without worry about quality. There will be no masterpieces here, but you just may find little treasures that you're excited to play around with later. Or, you may simply enjoy seeing what has come out and send it off to the recycle bin.

Either way, you get to wear the label "writer." It suits you.

Write on,
Kim

PS: If the fruits of this writing find a wider audience—at your blog, in a social media post, in an online literary magazine, or a book of your own—please drop me an email (kim@kimsuhr.com), so I can spread the word!

Bonus Prompt: Write your own origin story of being a reader and your relationship to books.

| 1 |

Inspired by "Jewel Tea"

Door-to-door salesmen (and, most often, they were *men*) were a fixture of a different era. Over time, women got in on the action selling to each other: kitchen gadgets, over-priced cosmetics, burping plastic storage containers, you name it. School kids, too, have been tapped to sell everything from candles to candy bars to wrapping paper. These prompts explore the things we sell to each other and how.

Fiction

Write a scene in which one character is trying to sell something to another one. Even better, include a subtext in which the scene is about "selling" more than just an object or service—maybe something emotional or interpersonal.

Nonfiction

Write about your own experience with person-to-person sales, either on the selling or buying end of the equation.

OR

Write an essay in which you discuss the experience of having to sell something. Was it character-building, soul-crushing…and/or something in between?

Poetry

Write a poem in which the poetic "I" explores the notion of a selling-buying relationship.

| 2 |

Inspired by "Latent"

Latent ['leI t(ə)nt]: adj: present and capable of emerging or developing but not now visible, obvious, active, or symptomatic.

~Merriam-Webster Dictionary

Humans are like archaeological sites: layers of experiences and beliefs covered over with newer and different experiences and beliefs. These prompts encourage you to consider what lies dormant and what might happen when these quiet ghosts reawaken.

Fiction

Write a scene in which a character recalls, rediscovers, or unearths something long-buried from their past and struggles with the decision to share or not to share it with another character.

Nonfiction

Choose some element of your life (professional, romantic, psychological, physical, etc.) and dig through the layers unearthing the *you*'s that came before. You might use the metaphor of an archaeological dig to ground the trip through different eras in your life.

Poetry

Write a poem in which you (or the poetic voice "I") call forth different versions of the self. Perhaps with a sonnet-like "turn"* in the final few lines.

*Also known as the "volta," the turn in a sonnet often begins with "but," "yet," or "however" and makes a dramatic shift from the main direction of the poem. It has the effect of awakening the reader to a different meaning or perspective.

| 3 |

Inspired by "Numbered Days"

We may not like to acknowledge it, but as mortals, our days on Earth are numbered—and our demise will most likely be from disease, accident, or old age. But what if our end comes in an unexpected, less "mundane" form? These prompts suggest looking at death sideways.

Fiction

Write a letter in the voice of a fictional character in their final moments before meeting their end in a mysterious, maybe even other-worldly, way. Consider to whom they are writing, what they want their final words to be, and why.

Nonfiction

People sometimes talk about the "death of a thousand cuts." What are the "cuts" that could ultimately do you in? This might be a "rant" piece in which you let off steam, or it could be a social commentary that addresses an issue (or many) that get(s) in your craw.

Poetry

Write a list poem in which you name all the things in life that conspire to "kill" us. You might group the items on the list by category. The final stanza could be your commentary on the whole thing. (Try to give it a title that clues your reader in to the theme/tone of the piece.)

| 4 |

Inspired by "Only One"

According to *Psychology Today*, the term "medical miracle" suggests "events that are unanticipated and inexplicable, outside the range of medical precedents." Some people attribute these outcomes to divine intervention; others believe there is a scientific explanation that is, as yet, undiscovered. Either way, there is still plenty of mystery in the world of medicine and healing.

Fiction

Careful what your wish for! Write a scene or story in which the protagonist experiences a "medical miracle" with results that are vastly different from what they had expected. Be sure to weave in dialogue and setting details to put the reader there.

Nonfiction

Recount an unexplained turn-about in your health or a health-condition of a loved one.

Poetry

Write a list poem expounding on the things you'd like to understand—but don't: perhaps start with your own body and move outward in ever widening circles.

| 5 |

Inspired by "Pay Phone"

When pay phones arrived on the scene, they gave people a new power to connect with others remotely when away from home. The phones were a part of the public landscape for generations. These prompts encourage you to recall and explore this artifact, that many now consider a relic of the past.

Fiction

Write a story or scene in which a pay phone--or phones or other communication devices--play a pivotal role in the outcome.

Nonfiction

Write a "word slideshow" of as many brief recollections of pay phones from your life as you can recall. Maybe number them from 1-9 (like the numbers on a keypad) with the final section—zero—being your "today voice" looking back on what you have just shared.

Poetry

Write a 10-stanza numbered poem (again, like the keypad on a pay phone, you could add in a stanza for the * and # keys, too) with brief glimpses of different pay phones.

OR

Write an ode to the pay phone.

| 6 |

Inspired by "Pretty People"

When we're in high school, the impressions we form of people—of *types* of people—are strong and sometimes indelible. It's easy to forget that no one keeps in their 17-year-old personality for their whole life. These prompts encourage you to look through your (or a fictional adolescent's) eyes and then through the eyes of an adult.

Fiction

Write a scene at a class reunion in which two characters see each other after a long absence and an old misunderstanding is (or isn't) addressed. Be sure to add setting details to put yourself deep into the scene.

Nonfiction

Recount bumping into someone from your high school years (this could be in person or on social media). Include necessary backstory from "then" to explore your reaction to them now.

Poetry

Write a two-stanza poem in which stanza one captures a "time ago" with someone (friend, foe, frenemy, stranger, teacher/coach) and stanza two conveys who you (or the poetic "I") are now.

| 7 |

Inspired by "Blank"

O ften, the days that change our lives begin in a hospital: childbirth, surgeries (successful and not), final words, final breaths. These prompts explore those pivotal moments.

Fiction

Write a dialogue between a medical professional and a patient or family member. Remember that the words characters say are only part of the communication. Body language and gesture often say more than their words. Maybe have one or the other of them not being completely forthcoming with the other.

Nonfiction

Write about an experience you had in a hospital setting either as a patient, family member, or medical professional. For a new perspective, talk about yourself in the third person as if you are a distant observer of the scene rather than in the first-person, close perspective.

Poem

Brainstorm as many words having to do with the hospital as you can think of and then write a poem, each stanza of which beings with a different "hospital" word.

| 8 |

Inspired by "Play-School"

Children's pretend play reveals much about the things that are on their minds—their hopes, their fears, their fascinations. We have all been children, but many of us have lost the ability to immerse ourselves in the make-believe. These prompts encourage you to go back to your child-mind.

Fiction

Write a scene completely in the point of view of a child as they "work through" some adult problem. Consider what toys or other items they might incorporate into their play and how they will use the objects.

Nonfiction

Revisit your favorite pretending game as a child, in as much detail as you can remember. Either along the way or at the end, weave in your adult analysis of what the "little you" was trying to learn or work through.

Poetry

Write a rhyming poem (with rhythmic meter would be even better) in which you explore some element of your childhood play. Maybe one stanza for each different game you loved or focus on one for the entire poem.

| 9 |

Inspired by "Rink Rat"

A child's world is peopled with a variety of adults: teachers and coaches, neighbors and relatives. Some are central while others may seem to be peripheral. These prompts ask you to consider the "bit players" whose influence ends up shaping kids' lives beyond expectations, and, perhaps, without their knowledge.

Fiction

Write a scene or story in which a character "steps from the sidelines" to influence another in a profound way.

Nonfiction

Brainstorm a list of the adults who shaped you in big—and small—ways as you were growing up. Choose one and write them a letter recalling in as much detail as you can the moments in your relationship that affected you most. (If they're still around... send it!)

Poem

Write 8 flashes (simple phrases or images) of memory about a person who shaped your development. Number the lines from 1-8 and plug them into the formula for a pantoum-like* poem. Enjoy the effect of juxtaposed lines bumping up against each other and the echo effect of repeated lines.

Pantoum-like Template (each stanza has 4 lines corresponding to the numbered flashes)

Stanza 1: 1, 2, 3, 4

Stanza 2: 2, 5, 4, 6,

Stanza 3: 5, 7, 6, 8

Stanza 4: 8, 1, 7, 3

*Pantoum: A Malaysian form of oral poetry that features repeating lines. It achieves its meaning and music through repetition and juxtaposition of the lines. Originally, pantoums also followed a prescribed rhyme scheme.

| 10 |

Inspired by "The Dip"

This section is made up of pieces written in a variety of forms that all "add up" to tell a story. Try these different vessels for conveying stories of your own.

Inspired by "Between Us and Our Friend"

Tell a story (real or made-up) using a series of text messages, emails, or written notes.

Inspired by "Ode to My Boobs"

Choose a published poem and use it as a model for a poem of your own. (You could blank out some of the words and add your own.) If you want to link the pieces in this section, choose one of the characters from the previous writing exercise to be the "poetic I" of the poem.

Here are some good poems to use as jump-offs:

- "Ode to My Socks" by Pablo Neruda
- "13 Ways of Looking at a Blackbird" by Wallace Stevens
- "Blossom" by Mary Oliver
- "This Is Just to Say" by William Carlos Williams

Inspired by "No Politics"

In a play script or screenplay format, write a scene in which 2-4 characters (perhaps from one of the previous writing prompts) find themselves in an "apart-from-daily-life" setting. The story must be told primarily through dialogue with only basic stage directions and actor cues (no internal dialogue allowed).

Inspired by "Prayer Bank of America"

Tell a story through a series of social media posts: through consecutive posts by one person or through posts & comments from others.

Inspired by "In Memoriam"

Write an obituary for a character that includes hints at "untold stories" in their background.

OR

Write your own obituary—a serious one or one that "plays" with the form by exaggerating, satirizing, joking, etc.

Inspired by "Unauthorized"

In play script or screenplay form, write a scene following a funeral or celebration of life in which the characters process the service they have just experienced. Characters may be close friends of the deceased or "thrown together" by circumstances. Perhaps there is a scene like this from your own life. The tone may be heavy or light or ridiculous.

| **11** |

Inspired by "Eradicated"

This story imagines what would happen in a world that finds creativity dangerous and in which people have willingly given it up—a la Ray Bradbury's *Fahrenheit 451,* the classic novel set in a world where society has criminalized books. "Eradicated" is also about a man rediscovering his latent creativity and forging his own private, quiet rebellion.

These prompts invite you to revisit the creativity of youth and, possibly, explore how one might regain it.

Fiction

Write a scene in which a character is engaged in some sort of creative pursuit in the physical world and infuse their actions with references, flashbacks, and interiority about a significant event in their life. Let the two different elements "talk to each other" in the scene.

Nonfiction

For 7 minutes, freewrite about the things that captured your imagination and activities in which you lost yourself as a child. Then write a "manifesto" in which you reclaim your creative self. Be sure to envision what your creativity in adulthood will look like and how it will manifest in your day-to-day life.

Poetry

Write a poem with alternating voices: Odd-numbered stanzas in the voice of a child (yours or the poetic "I"); Even-numbered stanzas in the voice of the grown child looking back. Explore some form of creativity—pursued or lost.

ABOUT KIM SUHR

Photo by Suvi Tori

KIM is Director of Red Oak Writing and leader of the prompt writing group, *Time to Write!* She holds an MFA from the Solstice Program in Boston where she was the Dennis Lehane Fellow in Fiction. Her story collections, *Close Call* (2024) and *Nothing to Lose* (2018) both from Cornerstone Press, unveil emotion in tight spaces, hearts in turmoil, and the searching soul of the Midwest. You can learn more about her at kimsuhr.com